Mengue m'Anaba Eka Abila

"If you ever doubted God's divine plan for your life just a few passages from this book will immediately change your mindset. Pastor Mengue proves that no weapon formed against us shall prosper. What a riveting account of one woman's journey of good triumphing over evil."

Rev. Pamela L. Ward,
CEO, *Redeemed Outreach Ministries*
Rosedale, New York

"This is a tremendous story of God turning the life of a victim into that of a victor in Christ! Reading her honest and incredible account, you will be convinced of God's promise to be so real that what is impossible with men is possible with God. If you have been suffering, and are now ready to give up, or if you are a discouraged woman in spiritual leadership, this book is for you."

Minister Sumi Han

"Pastor Mengue has risen from poverty, abuse, and depression to newness of life in the Risen Christ. Through her fearless discipleship Christ has led her to a victorious spirit in livelihood, education, and pastoral ministry."

John Hamilton
Follower of Christ, Pastor, teacher
Ordained Baptist minister 1968
D.Min., Southern Seminary, 1984

FORGET

THE WORD

EASY

FORGET

THE WORD

EASY

In the Beginning (Jesus was the Word), and the
Word was with God, and the Word was God.
John 1:1

"I could not afford not to forgive! I would have died young
and in bitterness..."

MENGUE M'ANABA EKA-ABILA

TATE PUBLISHING & *Enterprises*

Tate Publishing
& Enterprises

Tate Publishing is committed to excellence in the publishing industry. Our staff of highly trained professionals, including editors, graphic designers, and marketing personnel, work together to produce the very finest books available. The company reflects the philosophy established by the founders, based on Psalms 68:11,

"The Lord Gave The Word And Great Was The Company Of Those Who Published It."

If you would like further information, please contact us:
1.888.361.9473 | www.tatepublishing.com
Tate Publishing & Enterprises, llc | 127 E. Trade Center Terrace
Mustang, Oklahoma 73064 USA

Scripture quotations are from the *New International Reader's Version,* Copyright © 1996, 1998 by International Bible Society. Used by permission. All rights reserved.

Published in the United States of America

ISBN: 978–1–6024730–2–7

07.03.06

Special thanks to the following people for all their contributions to the drafting, editing, and other leading contributions to this publication:

Alexis Godonou, Lauren Canning, Maxime Allonce, Guy Eyebe, Ruth Engo, Emilienne Ze Ononino, Normand Lauzon, Raphael Ebanga Mballa, Metende Mbarga Manga, Deborah Botham.

ABOUT MENGUE M'ANABA EKA-ABILA

Mengue was born in August 1957 in Yaounde, Cameroon, to male nurse Timothée Eka-Abila, and Dorothée Anaba Mengue. She has two adult sons, Timothée and Joseph.

Former International Civil Servant of the United Nations Development Programme, New York, she holds a Certificate in Christian Ministry from the New York Theological Seminary, a B.A. in Psychology from Hunter College, and an M.S. in Rehabilitation Counseling from CUNY.

Raised a Roman Catholic, this multilingual, multicultural, and impassioned music lover and performer, was called in the Ministry of the Gospel at the age of 20 in Cameroon (West Coast of Africa). Officially licensed 19 years later in the First Baptist Church of Brownsville, Brooklyn, NY, by Bishop a.d. Lyon, she was ordained 27 years later by Bishop Stephen A. Thomas, Community Fellowship Church of Ministries, Inc., Dalton, Georgia.

Founding Pastor of Helper Ministries International, Inc., Mengue also worked as a volunteer in the Protestant Chaplaincy of Bellevue Hospital, Manhattan, New York.

Pastor Mengue M. Eka-Abila
Helper Ministries International

P.O. Box 170605
Brooklyn, New York 11217
www.helperministries.org

E-mail: mengue@helperministries.org.

TABLE OF CONTENTS

FOREWORD

Mengue Eka-Abila is a monumental testament to the power of sheer faith in God's ability to use her life as a mirror in pursuit of destiny and purpose. She came from Cameroon, Africa, to New York with $150, a Bible and many scars inside and out.

As I read and re-read this wonderful book I couldn't help but think about Job. Those of us who feel that we have endured hardship, ridicule, and abuse will see that nothing could possibly compare to this unshakable spirit.

I can guarantee you that your life will never be the same upon completion of this book. What an honor it is to know this preacher of the Gospel. She calls me friend. WOW! Pastor Mengue is an extraordinary woman and humanitarian.

Once you begin reading this spellbinding account of unbelievable events you will be unable to put it down. Today I not only celebrate this God's woman but I salute the awesome power of God which sustained her through every storm.

~Elder Bernice Jamison-Turner
Assistant Pastor~ Pleasant Grove Tabernacle
Brooklyn, New York

INTRODUCTION

Some among us have given up any hope of knowing a richer existence, but many people who had long abandoned any hope to see a better life have found peace, joy, dignity, and strength by faith in God through Jesus Christ our Lord and Savior. Their faith, courage and enormous sacrifices inspired hundreds of thousands of people. In the same way, you can choose to say "NO!" to defeat. Your life *can* be changed! You have been created to be happy, to prosper, to exercise dominion and not to be dominated by anything. In Jesus' name.

To forgive is the beginning of all re-births from humiliations, inhuman treatment by oppressive and abusive persons and control systems. To dare to understand the flaws of human vision and dynamics is part of the process.

We were all created in the image of God. To be dominated by our fellow humans is simply unacceptable. This narrative is a painful duty of memory, the heart cry of a woman of faith against her crushed destiny, guided by the courage to forgive, even when the pain was still sharp.

Jesus Christ keeps on liberating the prisoners and other outcasts!

HAPPY BEGINNING

Mengue m'Anaba Eka-Abila, daughter of Eka Abila, a male nurse, and Anaba Mengue, a multitalented housewife, granddaughter of Abila Assomo Ngoa Meyobeme Amieh Ntolo, all Beti.

A significant portion of my childhood evolved in the village of Ntu Essong, Baaba, now a suburb of Yaounde. My parents were easy going, good-looking, ambitious, and achievers. They were the pride of the family in the African sense of the term. Mom was a great seamstress. She sewed beautiful dresses and embroidered pieces, and knitted some of the best sweaters I had ever seen. She was also an excellent cook.

They were well known in the community for their social status, their physical beauty, and also for their kindness. My father administered nursing services in the community for free. In addition, they owned a car (a Renault L4), a rare commodity in our community in the post-colonial environment of the 1960s. Our compound extended over almost 16,000 sq. ft.

We had four houses, two big ones, one medium one, and a kitchen house with two bedrooms, the sleeping quarters of the paternal and maternal grandmothers. The pig stall was located on the east side of the compound, behind the medium house. The south side of the compound accommodated the sheep and goats under a big safu tree. The same area was also filled with banana and plantain trees, papaya and custard-apple (eboam) trees, along with tomatoes and other useful plants. The house by the street side was put to rent for a while. My parents were highly respected by many in the community. Moreover, my parents loved and respected each other, and I was proud them.

At the risk of disappointing my eight other brothers and sisters, I had a particular admiration for my elder sister. She was extremely bright, protective, caring, very well behaved and tidy. She was also hard-working and particularly demanding with regards to personal hygiene!

In those days, it was customary for some parents to send their offspring on vacation or for a longer stay to the grandparents in the village. Apart from missing my parents whenever I stayed in the village, I was quite happy. We were a blessed family.

This is where most of my cultural immersion and shaping took place. The training was done through observation of, and participation in, the evening activities of lively Beti rituals, dramatic telling tales and legends.

The oratorical style was made of eloquent philosophical words, proverbs, gestures, songs and beautiful dance steps at times enthralling, and frightening at other times. I learned of Kulu, the Tortoise, with his cunning strategies, and Ze, the Panther, the fool who always fell victim to Kulu's schemes. Beme, the Pig, was simple in his thinking and lazy, always trying to imitate someone else instead of thinking for himself, and constantly failing, but never learning. One of my favorite stories was the story of Mengue m'Eyenga, the orphan girl, raised and maltreated by the wicked stepmother and her mean children. But she later on marries a great king, and her former enemies become subject to her. There were also war stories of the exploits of our great heroes such as Mintodo, the war name of my father's (Mintodo Mi Ngele) namesake (who was so ferocious in war that his smell changed while in battle), Ngoa Abomo, Si Meko'o, Ngoa Evina, and other historical figures. Other stories told of how our ancestors had originally come from beyond the Sanaga River, and crossed the river on Ngangmedzaa, the benevolent giant snake, and the genesis of the Beti People, whose ancestor was Nanga Beti.

Most stories were concluded with philosophical proverbs that gave us a better understanding of the general and specific ideals of our ancestral mythology and history. I cannot forget the festive women fishing parties (alök), and anatomy lessons disguised in songs in the evenings, whereby we recited the names of the different body parts of Nkaa, the Pangoline, or the various groups of animals, those with tail and those with no tail. The song was supposed to be sung by Nyogo'o, a tail-less animal who felt sorry for itself for not having been endowed with a tail. In the same way, we were made to recite the names of the different fishes of our streams and rivers.

I spent my first years of study at the Roman Catholic Missionary School of Nkol Melen, Baaba. In the believing, practicing Roman Catholic Community, the first communion ceremony was a special event. My turn came naturally at the age of seven. My parents organized a great celebration that lasted almost one week. On each of the first three days, there was a reception for a different set of people. The First Communion itself took place in Nkol Melen after which there was a small reception at my aunt's house in Nkol Lembe, not far from the mission center. A dear friend of my father's, Papa Pas Edzengede, drove him to the village in his own car to fetch me. We left the village for the city, where there was a bigger celebration. No invitation cards were necessary. There was more than enough food, and anybody who felt close enough to my parents was welcome. My First Communion dress was all white and beautiful, and the lovely white crown stood apart from all the other jewelry. My dress and my white leather shoes (slipped over decorated white socks) had been imported from France. My white handbag held nothing but a few pieces of candy and an exquisite white handkerchief.

My mother made the other outfits, quite a project for this special week. Altogether, I donned two different outfits the first day. After the dinner, I put on another new dress. On the following days, I wore a different outfit everyday.

On Monday, there was a special reception for my father's colleagues. Tuesday's reception was for some neighborhood and community dignitaries. I relished the attention I was getting. There was lots of food and drinks, live music, mainly mendzang and kwe, and lots of singing and dancing, all of which was traditional and beautiful, according to the Bantu code of practice. People talked about my great dancing skills, stuck cash (bills) on my face, threw cash at me, in the basket or on the ground at my feet. It is a local tradition that well pleased watchers encourage dancers (or singers and musicians) by throwing money at them or rubbing it on the dancer's face to wish them luck. The few who did not have cash gave me live chickens after dancing around me while brandishing the fowl in the air. This was also supposed to bring me "good luck."

My aunt became my de facto treasurer, although she did not account for all of my money. This became a big topic of discussions in the family after the feast. I was not aware of the value of money at the time. All I knew was that I received lots of attention, adulation, and money. Whatever she bought for me was just fine.

THE SEEDS OF EVIL

My parents were peaceful people. They hated conflicts, quarrels and fighting, and it was forbidden in our home. Nothing was bad enough to warrant a fight. If your older sister or brother hit you, you did not hit back. You reported the matter to the parents or to one of the adults present in the compound.

Human nature being very complex, the prosperity of our family started to arouse envy. When I was almost thirteen, my happiness began to take deadly blows. Not everybody was delighted to see my family prosper. Bad things began to happen to both my family and to me. Some students from the Baaba, Kong, and Vö-2 schools, a mean-spirited bunch, beat me up without provocation. They mocked me and made provocative comments about certain parts of my body. They seemed to seriously enjoy this malicious exercise. Those became the dark years of my childhood.

By that point, my mother had made up her mind that any time there was a problem, I had started it. I had been somewhat hyperactive as a younger child, and had indeed started a few fights in those years. My parents, peaceful as they were, had been concerned by my hyperactivity. With this background in mind, I did not bother to report the abuse to them. I was not fighting back either. I became depressed and psychologically disturbed. I endured humiliations and mockeries without crying or complaining. These were turned into a childhood nightmare. I became so depressed I lost those two academic years, and repeated the grade. Around the same time, I faced my first instance of sexual abuse.

I insist on our religious dogma for a better understanding of the reasoning of the girl child that I was. Without trying to clear myself of some of my incomprehensible silences, my wounds of the soul conceal mysteries and unvoiced comments, but when one comes from a deeply believing and insufficiently informed family, one can be disarmed in front of the inhumanness of Humankind. Mine was a devout Roman Catholic family. My mother and grandmothers were in the Legion of Mary. No one in my immediate environment ever took a critical look at our religion. It would have been construed as blasphemy. Sexuality was taboo in my family. One did not especially call things by their name.

The Assistant Principal of the school of Kong, a priest (he was a national of a neighboring country), came to my class one day, and ordered me and some other children to go to his office. He was a Bantu man of about 37 years, average size, very dark and slender. An influential man, his very presence caused both calm and fear among the pupils. When we arrived at his office, he called us in individually, and made sure that I would be the last child called. When my turn came to step in, his tone of voice changed suddenly, saying very softly while pulling me towards him, "I want us to become friends..." and he began to fondle me. I was in the seventh grade at the time. I had no visible breasts. My hair was constantly shaven. I was without defense in front of this powerful stranger. For a moment, I was paralyzed with fear. I understood that what he was doing was not normal. It was clearly a sexual act, and that this was not supposed to happen. Fear hit me in the stomach like a hammer.

The ringing of the bell signaling the end of the ten o'clock break gave me the impetus to pull myself out of his grip and run back to my class. But by the time I got back to the class, I was traumatized. I was also confused. As a devout Roman Catholic, I knew a priest was a holy man of God. Therefore, I did not blame the priest. Rather, I blamed myself, thinking, "What is it in me that made this man of God do what he did to me?" This worsened my depression. I became absent minded, and spent most of my time daydreaming. I became withdrawn. Nothing was fun anymore. My sleep was filled with nightmares. I was divided between hatred and fear. Wasn't a priest a saintly man in the service of God? Wasn't I guilty? Did I have the right to blame a saintly man?

My parents noticed that something was wrong with me, and they were worried, but they never knew what had caused such distress to my personality. They probably thought it was the beating by the "bad kids", so they took the matter to the children's parents. This did not improve my mood. All their protection and attention did not have any significant benefit to my state of mind and heart.

My parents' decision to send me to Uncle L. Nakunu was inspired by God Himself. He was the principal of the Roman Catholic Primary School of Nkol Nkumu, a few kilometers into the then Yaounde-Douala dirt road. He always took time to listen to me every time I had a problem with anybody, child or adult. His understanding and love helped me recover from my depression quickly.

Uncle Nakunu had one wife whom he obviously loved a great deal. They loved each other, and played together as if they were kids. They had three young children at the time. The village people and the environment were very friendly, and I quickly became a happy young girl once again. Uncle N's real love and understanding had a magic effect on me. I became assertive again, and my school grades improved significantly.

The abrupt transfer of my uncle from Nkol Nkumu to Vö-2, a village not so easily accessible, was a low blow from his employers. Not only was the dirt road to this village poorly maintained, thus making it almost inaccessible by car, especially during the rainy season, there were no houses for teachers to rent. Consequently, the teachers from this school system depended on the hospitality of the people of the village.

Was my lack of enthusiasm premonition, with regard to moving to Vö-2 Village? In any case, a great part of my destiny as a woman was played there. Looking back, it amazes me how I got over the repeated sexual abuse I suffered in this village from the entire family (their two teenaged children who lived in the city excluded) that hosted us there. I will later consider the faith and the related spirituality, which enabled me to be restored.

Left in the claws of the family that lodged us, I suffered unimaginable traumas. Uncle Nakunu never knew that our host abused me sexually. This man was one of the notables of the Village. He owned a three-house compound: the big house, his mother's house in the middle, and his wife's big kitchen behind his mother's. I and my uncle's wife and young children were under the care of our host's wife during the daytime. I did my house chores in her kitchen house. Occasionally, I would be asked to help at his mother and sister's house instead. I was sleeping at the host's mother's and his divorced sister's house. With their complicity (they opened the door for him in the middle of the night while my uncle slept), he would come when his wife traveled far from the village, and would wake me up, first making the hush sign, then commanding me to follow him, and I would find myself in his marital bedroom. He would then talk to me in a "friendly" tone of voice. The disgust for these despicable acts prevents me from giving you more details. This happened at least twice.

The host's wife, who probably never knew what her husband did to me, also took advantage of my uncle's trust. On Saturdays, there were no classes. She would take me to work and fetch food in her farms up in the hills. It was during one such occasion that she brought her husband's older nephew to use me in a bush near their cocoa plantation. Prior to this, she had brought another man (not a direct relative of theirs) to abuse me sexually. One evening, my uncle's wife had traveled, and we were sitting and talking in her kitchen house. One of the men in the village called her outside. She stepped out for a few minutes. When she came back, she asked me to step outside the house, because someone wanted to talk to me. What transpired is too disgusting for any further description. She had turned me into a sexual object for the men of the Village, and insured unsuspected access to me.

The host's younger nephew, who lived with them, also abused me sexually and physically (more frequently). One evening, he, too, brought one of the teachers of the public school system of the village, to also abuse me sexually.

Rape is an inhuman act. For the victim, it is worse than a deep wound, it is a stain of the soul, a brutal invasion of one's intimate being with total disregard to the horrors being inflicted. The after-effects are multiple: a deeply wounded spirit with feelings of insecurity and helplessness, intimacy reduced to carnality, and saddest of all, the assurance of scars carried for the rest of the victim's life.

For most women, virginity is the subject of a great personal pride, the blue-chip/stock of femininity. While a virgin, you dream of the ideal man, that special man with whom you will be insanely in love, and to whom you dream to offer your heart and virginity. And suddenly, some other unwelcome man (or men for some), a stranger or an acquaintance, steps on all this, crushes your dreams and feelings, your very soul, with malicious delight, and walks away laughing at your expense! And you are scarred for life. My emotions as I write this section of the story make me understand how painful it is to forget so deep a wound, which will haunt you all your life. For those who suffered the same trauma, to share my story with you is also to help you toward recovery. Yes, recovery is possible in Jesus Christ. He is the only one who can cure the wound of the heart or soul.

I did not report these things to my uncle because sex was implicitly a taboo subject in our environment. Besides, if I had reported the abuse to my uncle, it would have put us in a more precarious situation. We were strangers in a hilly village that saw a truck passing only rarely. Things were made worse during the rainy season because the poorly maintained old feeder roads got too muddy and slippery, even for the adequately equipped cocoa and coffee beans buyers' trucks.

In spite of all this ugliness, Uncle N's love and understanding were such a boost that I managed to numb myself to my humiliations and pain, and feel as if I were happy again. I now realize that it was repression and self-deception, managing to deceive myself that I was still virgin.

In an emergency move, Uncle N decided to send me back to the city before the end of the academic year. He simply explained to me that some people were bothering him because of me, that is, they were asking him permission to marry me. He never told our hosts that I was leaving the village for good. He told them that I was going to visit my parents in the city for a few days, which was very wise of him. I can only guess that the harasser was our host. Uncle N had made an arrangement with Uncle B. Awuma, Principal of an all girl Roman Catholic primary school in the city, for me to complete my academic year there. Uncle Awuma took care of my registration for both the school and the exam. It was through that school that I passed my First School Leaving Certificate with flying colors. God bless Uncle Awuma!

Uncle N intervened in my life at the right moment and succeeded in giving it a direction. Had it not been for his effective support, I wonder what would have become of me. Uncle Nakunu will remain a hero to me, and all my life, I will have him in high esteem.

Years later, I visited him before my departure for the United States. I made him a small gift, a token of my gratitude for the saving role he had played in my life and for his importance as a person to me. I intend to help at least one of his children.

Very modest as he was, he never even mentioned his kind gesture to me, neither did he ask for anything in return, in spite of my letting him know that I would be delighted to help. He was a man faithful to only one woman. His recent sudden death, apparently of heart failure, which could have been avoided, represents a very great loss for me.

FROM PUSH TO SHOVE

The return to my parents in the City turned out to be a series of more traumatizing experiences for me. After only a five month absence, I found that our dream compound had been razed while my father, who was hospitalized in a coma, was fighting the deadly effects of poisoning. Later on, he lost his prestigious job position. All he had left were his ten children. Prior to these events, there had been trouble between him and my mother, and they were separated. Thank God my father did not die this time, but we became poor overnight, very poor. The fact that my father was still alive, however, kept me happy. My mother also frequently visited us, and I visited her and my other siblings when she was living in town.

The presence of both parents is necessary for the emotional and psychological balance of children and especially of teenagers. The vacuum left by the absence of my mother, who had not taught me how to defend myself against the attacks from human predators, had probably contributed to it.

The demons of rape had broken loose against me. Although I managed to defeat some would-be rapists in the city, I was still raped again and again over the following years. I conceived my two sons from rapes perpetrated by two different men. The first pregnancy occurred when I was fifteen years old, at a time when a young woman does not fully understand the changes of her body. I met this 25-year-old man at a female neighbor's.

One week or so later, as I was going to the movies in the afternoon, I bumped into the same man in the street. I recognized him and greeted him the way as I had always greeted any acquaintance in the street. He insisted that I should go see his house just a couple of steps behind the one by the street. The next thing I knew, I was locked in his room. He raped me, I got pregnant, and my life turned into a living nightmare. My father was heartbroken and sued the man for statutory rape. Cameroonian law stipulates that this is a crime and liable to at least 10 years of imprisonment. However, the legal battle was short-circuited because the man bribed the investigators, who took me to the Police Station without my parents. I was forced to sign all papers under threats of harm. The truth is, I was frightened, and I did not even read what I was made to sign.

The statement said that I disavowed my father in the name of the "love" that I supposedly had for this man, the rapist. When my father read it, he became so angry he almost lost his mind. It broke my heart to see him so heartbroken and disappointed because of me. He felt betrayed, and I can understand that. All I could do was tell him that they had made me sign things that I did not say or know.

My mother, despite her disappointment, made great sacrifices to be able to be of assistance. She was determined to take an additional step to give me another chance. She returned to live with us just days before the childbirth, without which both my son and I would have certainly died.

The second pregnancy occurred approximately a year later. For a few months, I had believed in a friendly relationship with the man who sired my second child. An apparently pleasant and caring man at the beginning, he helped me by buying drugs for my first child and an occasional little pocket money, without insisting on having sex with me first.

When this new chapter opened in our relationship, he could not understand that I was frigid, and interpreted my cold attitude toward sex as not liking him. I subsequently decided to let him use my body, just to discover a few months later that he had infected me with an STD. I was annoyed with him and broke up our relationship.

A few months after our break-up, he saw me in the company of one of my teachers who had helped me to pay for the medical bills resulting from my infection; he thought he was entitled to feel jealous in the name of our past relationship. I held firm. He then proposed a "friendly" reconciliation. I easily fell in the trap, thinking that there would be no harm to a friends-only type of relationship. I dropped my guard. I was wrong.

He invited me to his place for the Easter Day. Although he was initially with many friends of his, within minutes and in a well-orchestrated way, I found myself with him alone. Raping me was so easy to him. There the pieces of my broken life that I was trying to mend were now reduced to dust. All hope of ever having a normal woman's life was gone.

My sense of hopeless loss and brokenness would be hard to describe. I knew I was going to get pregnant, but did not know what to do or whom to talk to.

My second pregnancy plunged me into despair. I had become skeletal in appearance, having more bone than flesh. My stomach rejected everything I ate or swallowed, including my saliva. I lost more than 66 pounds within three weeks. Nobody knew or guessed that I was once again pregnant. My mother suspected witchcraft.

I cannot explain the circumstances that had pushed my father to remain so cold, but I understand that his reasoning and knowledge did not equip him spiritually or psychologically to prevent or help with my situation.

As a young unwed mother of two with no education, it did indeed seem like I had no future. I was financially stripped. I was a failure and became a de facto lower class woman. However, although disappointed, my parents did not cease to love me. They continued to express their love and affection to me as much as they could.

GROWING DARKNESS

Ignorance and exclusion from knowledge is a sad reality. In the absence of accurate and honest information it is hard to reason. When one feels weak and uninformed, being an easy victim can become a grim daily reality.

My mother, not knowing what exactly my problem was, thought it best to fight her own way to save her daughter from the torment of what she believed to be witchcraft. A stranger passing for a traditional healer successfully convinced my mother that I was going to die if I did not leave the city immediately. That's how she entrusted me to him, thinking I would be safe in the hands of this so-called seer.

He took me to his village the next day to "treat" me and to "protect" me. The only treatment I received was from his wife, who made me drink a certain bark. It was very effective because, within the space of a few days, the vomiting ceased. However, to look after me was not the only concern for this man.

The son of his wife was faster than he and raped me while the "seer" was still planning his move. He broke into my room in the middle of the night, and, weakened from weeks of illness, when I tried to resist, he slapped me pitilessly and threatened to do worse if I tried to oppose him again.

This time, feeling humiliated and angry, I reported the case to his mother. I was shocked to learn that she and her son had already discussed my situation. She added that she wished her son would marry me.

All hope of escape was gone when she added her own threats, saying that I would get hurt if I ever broke up with her son. She then went on and declared to everyone in the village that her son had impregnated me. I was speechless with disbelief.

Never could I have imagined such a thing possible! I was kidnapped de facto. My mother visited weeks later. I informed her of all that had happened to me. She was furious. Unfortunately, she found out the same day that I was pregnant. Her anger then turned to bitterness. My poor mother lost any hope in me. In fact, she said bitterly, "... I perceive that you were born to be nothing!" My father, before this, had made the same statement. She gave up on me and left me there with these people who had become my captors, and returned to the city when they told her that I would be returning there one month later. It took her a while to recover from her bitterness. I do not blame her at all.

My elder sister had also expressed much love and support. Although she did not know how I had conceived these two times, she did not say anything discouraging and made some clothing for my first baby. I will be always grateful that, when I was pregnant for the second time, my sister gave me money, a contribution sandpapered out of her savings. Due to her outstanding performance and grades, she had managed to get into a vocational high school that granted scholarships to some of its brightest students. This represented a fortune to her at the time, probably months of saving coming from her tiny scholarship. She had noticed my efforts not to give up going to school, although each day I was sent home for failure to complete payment of my school fees.

The $10 that my sister had given me turned out to be the only school fees I paid during this academic year. Although I lost this particular battle, I will never forget that my sister had been the only one to risk her money on me that year. She never gave up on me! God bless her!

In the end, it became like a game, trying to remain in school in spite of the pressure of unpaid tuition. The Principal of the school had already shown flexibility by accepting my $10 as down payment for the tuition.

But when the cut-off date for payment of the remaining sum of $100 arrived, I was unable to honor it. The wife of the founder of the school had often witnessed my expulsions from the school. One day, she spoke to me and asked, "Miss, you've been expelled many times for failure to pay your school fees, but you keep coming! Do you think you're going to be taking classes just for free?"

I replied, "Please Madam, I would like to pay, but I do not have any money. Please don't send me home!"

She took a compassionate look at me and after a moment of reflection, said, "You may return to the classroom." She allowed me to attend classes for free for the remainder of the year! Although my dark circumstances seemed to prevail that year, I will never forget her kind gesture toward me.

INNER CONVICTIONS

Human nature hates emptiness; I had hit rock bottom. But in spite of my traumas, humiliations, and failures, I decided to hang on to the belief that I could still make it. I determined not to let my past dictate my destiny. Although the majority of people my age and even younger were now ahead of me, I decided to succeed through education.

First I had to get rid of the sorcerer-kidnapper who had invaded my life. He had devoured two of my invaluable years, holding me captive with his threats, intimidations and manipulations. This young man and his mother had declared that they would kill me if I tried to escape or break up. For two years, I lived in this fear, knowing they would act on their threats if I rebelled.

It took me a few months of reflection. During that time a caring friend, a former classmate, Ndo'oh became concerned with my completely dropping out of sight, and started actively looking for me. Her determination to find me gave me enough courage to fight to take my life back. In the end, I managed to escape.

Though my captors tried to execute their threats, they did not succeed. In hindsight, I realize it was the grace of God that prevented me from being killed. I then decided to return to school and registered in the same school as Ndo'oh (Señorita). We called each other Señorita because we had once taken Spanish courses together.

I had tried to sell cosmetics door to door in order to be able to pay for my tuition that year. Unfortunately, the money I made was not enough. It was back to square zero; with my unpaid tuition, I was sent home again.

I was mired in a trap of poverty and misery, stuck at the very bottom with no seeming way out. At this point, a friend I loved and respected suggested that I take to the "Poteau", meaning prostitution. I was shocked, but remained silent. I instinctively knew that this would be the last blow to my sons' self esteem in the future. It was unacceptable.

However, the realities of the dark abysses of misery, contempt and rejection made me vulnerable to the temptation of becoming the mistress of a "folded neck" or "sugar daddy" who were prone to seeking objects for their fanciful sexual desires. Some young women of my age and social group, with or without children, considered this type of individual a blessing.

This pressure was constantly present. But I saw things another way. I felt that I still had value despite everything. The idea that a married man, often father of several children, some of them my age or older than me, could be arrogant enough to claim control over my life because he assisted me financially, revolted me.

A pretty classmate with no child had such a man. He beat her up each time he did not find her at home. I remember having encouraged her to break up with him because he was swallowing up her youth and future; but Mister Folded-neck had too much influence on her. His beating was so persuasive that she never tried again.

Girls like her were always well dressed with expensive clothes and shoes. However, the majority of them never went far in their studies, so much so that they became dependent on these men who made them live beyond their real financial capacities.

A "beautiful" offer came to me from a government Minister. He was older than my father, with children older than me. He proposed to make me rent a beautiful apartment in an affluent district of the City. He promised me a car with a driver. I did not say a word; I felt so insulted. The other "nice" offer came from a younger, good looking, and apparently intelligent man. Initially, I enjoyed talking to him because he seemed to make sense. By then I was working.

One day after work, he offered to drop me at home. At the house, he took a seat in one of my modest pieces of furniture and throwing glances at my un-painted cement walls and my un-tiled roof, he pompously declared: "Your apartment looks quite nice, but I could make it look more beautiful and furnish it. Then it would become my second home." I felt insulted and silently decided to never talk to him again.

I finally understood the rules of the game: help with no strings attached was not a reality in my environment. I decided that I would rather be stripped, as I was indeed, and free than to be in what I viewed as comfortable slavery.

One day, after being sent home for failing to pay my school fees, my father surprised me. He gave me the money I needed to cover the remaining tuition. I was speechless with emotion. My gratitude was too deep to come in words.

This unexpected gesture of my father's brought some degree of happiness to my heart after a long period of nightmare. For me, this was confirmation that I still had a future. My enthusiasm and energy came back. I was more determined than ever to make it and become somebody. For this, no challenge would be insurmountable. The immediate challenge was to finish high school and go to the university, albeit tardily.

A few months after my father had paid for my school fees, he was returning from work with a friend who carried him on a motorcycle. Just 300 feet from our house, a drunk driver lost control of his car and hit the bike. My father bore the brunt of the shock.

He was first in a coma, then in critical condition. The man who had been such a kind and generous male nurse and who always flew to help others without ever expecting anything in return was now laying helpless on a mattress at the entrance of the emergency room of the Central Hospital of the city. Because of severe internal bleeding, he needed immediate surgery. Despite his life and death situation, the doctor assigned to operate demanded that I have sex with him first!

I begged this man to save my father first, and I would forever be grateful to him, meaning every word I said. But he never performed the surgery. Neither did he mince his words about his demands. I am aware of the seriousness of this statement: yes, this doctor left my father to die to punish me for resisting him.

While he was still in critical condition, I found the courage to beg, in the streets, for money needed to buy the many prescriptions, some of them on a daily basis, received from the medical students who were trying their best to treat my father. I also begged, in the streets, for blood donations for his transfusions.

Dad had been left to the care of poorly trained medical personnel who were incompetent in the face of his condition. By prescribing so many useless medications, they ultimately poisoned his failing body. By the time he died, we had a big box full of those drugs. The generosity of the people who donated money and blood was made useless. Dad died under my eyes, in my arms, and I was completely impotent in the face of this tragedy.

My only consolation was in passing my exam that year and giving him this delayed good news before he passed away. This distracted him from his excruciating pain for a short moment. How grateful I am to the Lord that my father died with the assurance that I was not a waste as he had initially believed.

My elder sister took responsibility for two of our eight younger siblings (she was already married and worked in the North part of the country). I was to take care of the remaining six, a load incompatible with my means; but in a family such as ours, solidarity is a virtue impossible to circumvent.

As I sank in my worst depression ever to that point, I lived my first demonstration of the reality of God, an epiphany of sorts.

My sense of bereavement and despair had resulted in a body so weak and a mind so worried that I could not sleep. The less I slept, the weaker I became. One day I suffered a serious fever that was nearly fatal. I began feeling like life was leaving my already ravaged body. My maternal grandmother, my namesake, and my younger siblings started screaming in their hopelessness. Grandma Mbom was rolling on the floor, totally horrified at what she was witnessing.

I remember the screaming irritating me, but there was nothing I could do to stop it. As I kept sinking into this hard to describe state, I heard another voice yelling towards me, asking me where I was going and ordering that I do not go there! It was just as if I had a say in this disastrous situation. This ejected me back to life. I was stunned. The first thing I did was to order my family to stop screaming so that I could digest what had just transpired and pray quietly.

Implicitly, I knew that the voice had been that of the Lord. I said a silent prayer, confessing to Him that I was completely overcome by this gloomy situation and asking Him for strength to get over it. It was around this time that Señorita, now Señora, helped me. Her husband was an important man in the Government. Through him, I was able to find a government job as bilingual secretary.

As a female, I felt the need to be loved, but the majority of the men I met only had sex in mind. Even when they said they wanted to marry me, I did not feel loved. Nor did their stated love translate into acts of love. Although Señora visited me when she could, she was very busy with her new status as housewife to a government tycoon. I felt at my loneliest and missed her sorely.

Later I discovered that certain neighbors had called me "the problem girl". I had responsibilities that were far above my age and means. Feelings of loneliness and despair were threatening to swallow me up. I tried my best to keep my sanity and dignity in spite of everything.

It was hard to make ends meet. I learned the importance of putting things in perspective and clearly establishing priorities: first my children's needs in a holistic sense; then those of my family made of Mother, the two Grandmas, and the younger siblings. I continued the tradition of sacrifice for, and dedication to, the family that my father had established and exemplified in his good and bad days. There was nothing he would not have done for his family. Out of love for him, I simply had to follow his example. I did not want to fail in this. Meanwhile, my personal relationship with the Lord grew, albeit with difficulties inherent with my ignorance and the lack of a spiritual support system.

THE AWAKENING

The loss of a parent is both a cruel and divine exercise. Before the death of my father, I had had the good fortune to come across a book entitled *A Message to the Youth* by Billy Graham. It took only a few pages of the chapter entitled "Remedy for Worries" to touch my spirit.

In this book I read that God was good, and that I could put Him to the test to see His goodness for myself. No one had to beg me to start right away; I had more than enough worries. After my experience of a direct demonstration of His reality and goodness, I started to try Him out in a new manner.

Armed with the good results that I obtained from my simple and direct prayers, I stopped addressing my prayers to Marie or any other Saint. I also stopped making ritualistic prayers. They had proven themselves to be completely ineffective in my life.

I then started to make requests to God for specific things such as, "Eternal God, please help me to succeed in my exam; my God, please provide for means of transportation; please provide food for us today, in the name of your Son Jesus Christ." I discovered that my needs were consistently met and in a miraculous way.

Towards the end of the year 1980, I met a group of believing Pentecostals. Most of them were young and about my age. I liked and admired the enthusiastic boldness that resulted from their personal relationship with Jesus.

They proclaimed Him to be alive and still able to cure and deliver today as He did during His earthly ministry, 2000 years ago. The call to discipleship, inviting individuals to give their life to the Lord, was thus made to me. Resisting such a call never crossed my mind; especially in line with the fact that I already considered myself a child of God.

In January 1981, Jesus Christ baptized me in the Holy Spirit. I repented of my sins and was later baptized by immersion. I then found myself evangelizing. I spoke to people about the reality of God. I was filled with joy and enthusiasm stemming from my new status as born again Christian. I was happy to operate in the ministry of evangelization and full of enthusiasm.

Nothing seemed too difficult for me to do for the Lord. This evangelization started to bear fruits. Through me, some people started to come to the church and invited Jesus into their hearts. I also showed a tendency to help people to better understand the Word of God by way of teaching. I organized prayers sessions at my house on Saturday evenings, with the simple aim of bringing relief to the sufferings of those who participated. I also started to visit the afflicted in their homes and hospitals.

The clergy began to feel uncomfortable with that, because these were some of the characteristics of a pastor. Later on I was told that, as a woman, I was not supposed to be a pastor. Had I been a male, I would have been properly mentored and most likely offered a scholarship in a Bible school or seminary. Unfortunately, I was a girl. They thought it was unbiblical for a woman to be a minister, especially not a pastor.

My goal was to help the suffering. This went on for about a year and half. Then I left this particular church because of repeated shameful behavior by the senior pastor and a number of his associates. After eighteen months of confusion and frustration with no church home, the Lord led me to take a special moment in prayer (January 1984). He began to open my spiritual eyes to see the major reasons for the ups and downs in my attempts to live a holy life. Mainly, I was relying on my inner strength, which was too limited for the spiritual challenges I faced. I began to understand that I would have to entirely surrender my will to the Lord in order to live in a way that is worthy in His sight. I then made up my mind to do just that. I understood that I was to definitely give up any outside of marriage sexual relationship, not by my own power, but by His Spirit alone. I cried out to the Lord for deliverance and strength.

At the time, there was a man in my life. He was positively unlike any man I had ever met. A mutual acquaintance had introduced us, and it was love at first sight. He was young and intelligent. He had all the attributes I desired in a man: self-confidence, nice and caring, yet strong and gutsy. We were fond of each other.

I told him about my decision to develop a more solid personal relationship with the Lord Jesus Christ, and serve Him for the rest of my life. This meant that I could no longer continue having intimacy with him, which I was not supposed to do in the first place. I was hoping that he would want to come with me in the Lord, but he got upset and left. I was hurt, but I decided to accept his decision. Out of fear of my own feelings for this man, I hid from him whenever I saw him coming my way the following years. I loved the Lord with all of my being, and I did not want this relationship, or anything else, to hinder me in any kind of way.

I must confess that, during my time of church-lessness, and in my attempts at escaping loneliness, I fell into some wrong company and was led to pornography. This later on made my efforts to return to pureness of thought and sexual abstinence a physiological war. This battle was constantly raging in me, but with help from the Holy Spirit, I did not yield to my impulses and addictions anymore. This renewed closeness to the Lord made things clearer in my mind. I was now able to see the ugliness of self-centeredness and sin, and the various ways in which the Devil used them to control mine and other people's minds, emotions, and behavior; thus making sexual abstinence and fidelity to only one sexual partner seem elusive. This awareness made me hate the world system because it is built to enhance and stimulate the very self-centeredness that makes us spiritually weak and increasingly separated from God, the very One who can deliver and protect us from the Enemy of our souls.

Through avid Bible reading, meditating, and studying, I began to understand God's big plan, and the next stage of it, the Rapture, which is pending. I began to earnestly pray that the Lord would come right away. He then told me that He was willing and ready to come, but His Church is far from being ready for Him. I was dismayed because the vast majority of the Church, all denominations included, seemed to live as if there is no such a thing as a coming Rapture!

Later on, the Lord also showed me the requirement that the whole world be given a chance to choose or reject Him, through evangelism, first. This made me increasingly aware of the enormity and complexity of the work required for this to happen. "Lord, where do I fit in this Grand Plan?" I asked. I just wanted to do something to help evangelize the world and help make the Church aware of the coming Rapture, and get ready for it.

GOD'S PLAN

In April of 1984, I met a wonderful Minister of God who encouraged me in the ministry. I told him that I felt a strong calling to serve the Lord in the front lines. I was not so sure of the geographical location of these front lines. All I knew was that I could not deny this overwhelming feeling. He then told me that, in order for him to take me seriously, I would have to first bring at least fifty souls to the Lord. I heard him, but since I was already evangelizing in the streets anyway, I just kept at it, and resumed hospital visitations and prayers with individuals who accepted my prayers. This man of God became a mentor to me. I learned a lot under his leadership.

His Bible classes, books and seminars, as well as my personal Bible study and meditation, gave me a better understanding of God's Great Plan for humankind, and how I personally fit in it. His support helped me greatly, in the sense that he took time to listen to some of my family, personal, or ministry difficulties. He would then suggest how I could arrive at solutions by reading specific scriptures, and applying them to the appropriate situation. He taught me how to overcome sleepiness and wandering thoughts during my personal devotions, through discipline. He really seemed to believe in me. Meanwhile, I lost track of our earlier conversations about my calling.

One day, toward the end of 1985, he surprised me with a promotion to church leadership. Days before this, he told me that he had observed that I was consistent in evangelism and bringing in new disciples. He then added, "You may now go ahead and feed them." I was very happy to hear him say that, but it did not occur to me that this was part of the process of official acceptance into the ministry.

My first invitation to attend our church leaders' meeting took me totally off guard. I had no idea the church leaders had been observing me. The reason why I was so surprised was that the abovementioned Minister acted more like a friendly big brother during our mentoring meetings. I did not see myself as a church leader at all. I thought of myself more as a flawed, albeit compassionate and friendly, individual. Now that I had a better understanding of ministry and its leadership, I certainly did not think I could fit the profile of a church leader. When I attended this church leaders' meeting, I felt like an earthworm among real people, and that they had invited me by mistake. I was overwhelmed by feelings of inadequacy.

About one year later, I was beginning to feel more comfortable because I began to understand that all I had to do to be a good leader was to recognize my unworthiness. The Lord would glorify His name by doing His work through me as a vessel washed by the blood of Jesus Christ.

Around the same time, this man of God confirmed his authorization for me to lead a house church. He even allowed me to baptize new members. That's how I had my first pastoral experience, although without a license or ordination. I took it as an awesome responsibility. This kept me praying and making sure I did not grieve the Lord in any kind of way. As I continued with street and door-to-door evangelism, the Lord kept adding to my little flock. This went on for one year and a half.

Then trouble started, quite suddenly. Some people brought an evil report about me to this powerful man of God. Unfortunately, he did not take the time to verify things with me. He just assumed that what he had heard was true. My once affectionate big brother and mentor was now just an authority figure. He distanced himself from me. This made me feel really small and insignificant again. I did not know what to do. I felt misunderstood and rejected. I would have tried reconciliation by explaining that it was just a misunderstanding, but events beyond my control kept happening. Eventually we went our separate ways.

No one else would accept me as a minister of God. So, I found myself pastoring this house church outside of any denomination or affiliation, without a license. It was then that I began to get a sense that my ministry would be hindered.

Meanwhile, I had found a well-paying job as a bilingual secretary with the most prestigious international organization in the world, the United Nations. With my new job, my salary was more than tripled within a period of three years. I began to accumulate some material wealth: fine clothes, a car, a piece of land in the city where I started building a small house. When I left the ministry of that great servant of God almost everybody began to put pressure on me, telling me to join a church because, as a woman, I was not supposed to be a pastor.

Two guest pastors from abroad, one from New York and the other from Paris, visited my house church and affirmed this view, strongly advising that I stop what I was doing because, they said, I was outside of God's will. I did what they wanted me to do; that is, I took my little congregation to the young, fresh-out-of-Bible-school pastor they had recommended and submitted to him.

Those who had recommended this pastor to me said he recognized women's ministry. But, before long, I found myself muffled—barred from the pulpit, ostracized, and bullied. He had put me in charge of the new members' class as its teacher for a while. Then he unceremoniously removed me from that position and put a young man in charge. He would say things like: "Although the Lord has some times used Sister Mengue as an evangelist, this does not necessarily mean she is an evangelist..." I felt wounded inside. The only thing he saw fit for me was to turn me into a Deacon-in-training.

After two years of this "training", graduation was still not in view. This, in addition to other adversities in my life at the time (due to poor judgment and bad decisions I had made, I was losing almost everything I had earned and accumulated), became unbearable to me. This pastor and other church leaders said my misfortunes were a result of my rebelling against God by putting myself in the ministry. Feeling wounded and despised, I became very depressed.

However, this time, I fought depression by speaking the Word of God to myself, with intense praying (mainly in tongues) and fasting, and praising and worshipping the Lord. That's when I discovered the power of these spiritual gifts and weapons as described in 1 Corinthians 14:4; Ephesians 6:10–18; and 2 Chronicles 20: 22–26. With all this adversity, I did not collapse. I grew stronger in spirit. As a result, I defeated one vicious heart attack, and a milder one shortly thereafter, in the name of Jesus. This happened during a particularly stressful night. The day before, I had accidentally lost expensive merchandise that I had bought for credit. Suddenly, I found myself in debt up to the neck, for nothing.

All leaders among Pentecostals and other Evangelicals, with the exception of one, Elder Emmanuel Tchoua, who often came to my church to encourage us with his teaching and preaching, were strongly discouraging me from pastoral ministry.

There was so much I did not understand. I was aware of my limited knowledge. How could I have been so naïve? Maybe people were right about my status as a woman in the ministry; maybe as a woman I should not have tried to preach at all? I felt that I needed to start afresh. So, I prayed to the Lord to give me a chance to start my life anew, hoping that I would not make the same mistakes this time. I then started looking for a way out of my country, through prayer.

I started applying for jobs in international organizations within Africa. When this did not seem to work out, I tried France by contacting a French acquaintance of mine I had met in Yaounde shortly after my father's death. He turned me down. However, God in His unfathomable wisdom led me to another nation, in another continent.

I then sent an application to my employer's Headquarters in New York, and waited quite a while for a reply. After sending a reminder, I received a letter offering me the option of a test, with the proviso that I would have to take care of my own transportation and lodging. A few weeks before receiving the reply from New York, the Lord clearly spoke to me, telling me that my assignment in my country was over, and that He was getting ready to take me some place else to serve Him there. I asked Him where that would be. He answered that I did not have to know at this time. So, when the letter came from New York, I knew that was where I would be serving the Lord next.

Being broke, I turned to the New York resident preacher, who had visited my house church in Yaounde twice, and for whom I had organized a few preaching engagements in different churches in two major cities in my country. The second time he visited, I had already resigned my pastoral position and surrendered to another pastor. This pastor, the church, and myself received him very warmly. He is one of the two pastors whose strong advice against my pastoral ministry had led to my above-mentioned move. All I wanted was that he put me up for a few days while I would be preparing for the test. He, too, declined. This disappointed me, but I knew the Lord would help me somehow. He did.

I arrived in New York on May 5, 1990, penniless, yet full of faith and confidence in my God. He put me in the hands of a good Samaritan, a Metropolitan Transit Authority (MTA) employee. God touched his heart for me. He contacted his father in East New York to ask him to put me up for the night. He readily accepted to host me.

Powerful gunshots woke me up around 2 a.m. that night. I was utterly shocked by this new reality. The only real gunshots I had ever heard, until then, were from hunters in the forest, at night, every now and then in the village, or at noble men's funerals, in my childhood. I had also witnessed the coup attempt in my hometown in April 1984. This was no hunting gun in the forest. It was not an African nobility funeral or war either. This was New York. After a few days, I understood that gunshots were a common occurrence in this neighborhood.

Four days later, I was rescued by a fellow African (DR of Congo), Manitou Kinzonzi, whose brother (a UN colleague) had given me a letter to hand deliver to him. I called his house to let him know about the letter. His wife Drusula, an African American, took the message for him. When she found out where I was living, she was most concerned and asked him to bring me to their home instead.

They put me up for two months. Their help, including transportation to and from the United Nations and church, advice, food, phone, and other basic necessities, was vital in preparing for the test. I will forever be grateful to them. God bless the Kinzonzi family! The staff of the Cameroon Permanent Mission to the United Nations was also most helpful and supportive. God bless them, too!

I finally passed the test after some difficulties and initially found short-term assignments (one-month, and two-months) as a bilingual secretary. With lots of hard work, discipline, and faith in God's help, I was able to move from short-term jobs to longer term ones, and finally a permanent contract about three years later.

Drusula Kinzonzi took me to her church, First Baptist Church of Brownsville, Brooklyn, the following Sunday, eight days after my arrival. Later on, I found that it was there that the Lord had prepared another man of God to hold my hand and show me the way. My Senior Pastor, Bishop a.d. Lyon, believed in me and licensed me as a minister of God in June of 1996. This event brought me to a new level in ministry.

Prior to this, I had sat in the pews for one whole year, determined to find out if my calling to ministry was really of God or of my own enthusiasm for the things of God. My thinking was that, if God really called me to ministry, He would have to prove it with some irrefutable signs before I ever get involved in the ministry again, especially in the area of preaching or teaching. If not, it was simple; I had suffered enough because of my involvement in ministry leadership, and I had no intention of perpetuating such suffering. So I sat down as a regular member at this church and kept my mouth shut. I enjoyed the African American Gospel singing so much that I joined the mass choir.

However, the Lord was not pleased with my attitude. So, he confronted me by reminding the reason why He had brought me in this city and this church.

He asked me if this was what I called serving Him. It was then that I started actively participating in the discussions of the New Members' Class. The teacher of this class, Sister Annie McCray, along with the Sunday School Superintendent, Elder Malcom Lane, did not hide their pleasure. They both loved the Lord. They immediately accepted me, and made me assistant teacher for the New Members' Class after a few months.

Meanwhile, I kept my determination not to talk about anything pertaining to my past experiences in the ministry, until one Sunday in June 1991, the unexpected happened. Namely, Sister Priscilla Lyon, the first lady of this Baptist church prophesied to me!

Sister P. Lyon had sent Sister D. Kinzonzi to ask me to join the Women's Ministry's prayer that morning. I readily accepted and followed her. Sister Lyon asked me to lead the prayer. Immediately after we closed the prayer, and during the general hugs, she just would not let me go, and said, "God has a work for you! God has a work for you! What an anointing! What an anointing!" Just days later, the same Women's Ministry organized a seminar at the Sheraton Hotel near JFK Airport. They made me one of the speakers, and put my presentation last. This was a mark of honor and trust. Not only did I teach the Word, I also disclosed my past pastoral experience to the audience. This was the confirmation I had been waiting for. God Himself had introduced me to this church as His servant. From that time on, I did not

MENGUE M'ANABA EKA-ABILA

66

care who said anything against women in ministry, or against me in particular. Curiously, at this point, open opposition stopped.

In 1992, Pastor Lyon appointed me Youth Director of his church. Again, there was opposition, but of a different kind. Some people had strong reservations about my being relatively new in the church, and thought someone with a more senior membership should have had the position. By the grace of God, the Associate Pastor and Minister McCray, along with Sister Kinzonzi (who had brought me to this church) backed the Pastor's decision and gave me all the support I needed to carry out my new responsibilities. After my licensing in 1996, my title was changed to Youth Minister. I received generally positive feedback from the Youth church, and the church at large. Later on, I became the Director of our church's Evangelism Ministry. My Sunday School teaching continued.

From April 1984, when I clearly heard and accepted God's call to ministry, to June 1996, when I was licensed as a Minister, it took twelve years. At long last, I was officially recognized as a Minister of Gospel. To get to this level, I had to first go to school for training: beginning with the theological seminary (New York Theological Seminary, Certificate Program) from which I graduated in June 1995; then the City University of New York (Hunter College) for a Bachelor of Arts in Psychology (June 1997); and a Master of Science in Rehabilitation Counseling (June 2001).

PSYCHOANALYSIS

Looking back over my life, I realize that, after having worked in the ministry in my country and in the U.S. for more than twenty years, the Lord has taken me through various experiences to prepare me for the work He had set aside for me to do. What a school! What a training! Definitely, it was the Lord who spoke to me back in 1986 when He told me to *"Forget the word 'easy'!"*

"For we are His workmanship created in Christ Jesus for the good works where unto He has called us into."
Ephesians 2:10

On the personal side, my growing understanding generated new questions in my mind. To better understand myself, introspection was needed. It was gradually dawning on me that my personal experience was unusual.

With God's help, I began to take trips into my inner world. Some traits in my personality, and external factors also, were becoming clear to me. For example, it occurred to me that I was compassionate and caring—nothing wrong with that—with good learning abilities, willingness and readiness to develop them. I was self-motivated. I tended to be enthusiastic about the things I liked. I was also outgoing. Most people said I was good looking and attractive. Namely, my lighter complexion and thick hair texture (abui esil) attracted men in my community.

Unfortunately, I was also physically weak and mentally unprepared. All it took at the time was a twist of my arm or a slap on my face to neutralize me. Naïvete was pervasive—I tended to look only at the positive side of people, and displayed readiness to trust people in general. Also, it was hard for me to scream when facing danger, and call for help. I concluded that this combination of naïvete, stoicism, physical attractiveness, and physical weakness, was the fateful mixture that had made me such easy prey to the system. "What to do?" I asked myself. I was in emotional turmoil. There had to be a way to change this deadly combination.

How did I learn to trust so easily, to be so naive? Why was sexual assault so frequent, so easy with me? Why was it so difficult for me to cry out, to scream, like others, when facing danger? How did I get to be this way? Could my life have been any different? Why was I so physically weak? Did I have to be strong to be treated with respect? Was my physical attraction a curse?

I took more painful inner trips. I was sick with anemia, low blood pressure, palpitations and cardiac arrythmia. I frequently visited the doctor's office. All medical tests and examinations were negative. One doctor advised that I was not sick. This made me upset and depressed. Then my hair began to fall out mercilessly, leaving spots of baldness in the front and the back of my head.

Meanwhile, some interesting answers to the questions I had asked myself about my own behavior began to take shape. While revisiting my early childhood environments (city and village), I noticed two communities of generally responsible individuals and families.

The adults of my childhood were not perfect, but they made taking their individual and collective responsibilities a highly valued prize. Being caring, giving, respectful, respectable, and sociable were strongly encouraged. Dignity, humility, and modesty were also high on the list of moral values. For the most part—not always—people were held to their words. As an oral tradition community, words were very important; i.e., those with the tendency to say things for the sake of saying them were not respected. This was a disincentive for me to lie deliberately, and an encouragement to believe that people meant what they said, and said what they meant.

In the village, there was only one notorious family of thieves, and one accursed, single man who did not bother to marry, but he specialized in taking married women from their husbands. Murder was a rarity; I only remember two. The first in the village was disguised as a hunting accident, and the other, in the city, was a murder attempt. One man made his bigger and taller victim drunk, and tried to strangle him to death in the middle of the night. These two events were talked about for a very long time.

Three women had been caught together stealing a stem of plantains. Because stealing was strongly discouraged in our culture, they were automatically put in songs that were sung at weddings and First Communion celebrations everywhere in the area. One man was so greedy he walked around with a spoon in his bag, so no one would use lack of spoon as an excuse to not invite him to share their dinner. He too was put in songs. The songs would incriminate both the culprit and his or her clan. The culprits were despised both in and outside their clan.

Children were so precious that, when things did not work out between the parents, both mother and father, with the support of their respective families, would fight for custody of their children. Those who did not have any children were usually consoled with children of their relatives. One had to have a child.

Most couples were married: traditionally, legally, and or religiously. Male single parents who had not at least traditionally married—mainly due to severe poverty—had no reason to be proud of themselves, because their might-have-been in-laws could claim and take away their children at any time. A marriage without the dowry, namely the bride price (eveka), comprised of gifts in kind and cash to the bride's family, was not considered a real marriage because marriage was between families, not just two individuals. All members of the groom's family contributed shares to the dowry. On the traditional wedding day, the bride's family, including all close and distant relatives, would have all the gifts (angada) ready for their daughter and sister. The more expensive and complete the angada, the greater the prestige and respect for the bride and her family in her in-laws eyes. Such marriages were very hard to break.

Most men, my father in particular, treated their wives with respect and the wives lavishly returned the favor. Women sang the merits of their husbands at feasts. Because most people had embraced Christianity, there were few polygamous families. I remember two close neighbor polygamous families in the city: each man took a second wife when all hope was lost for the first wife to ever bear a child. The first wife was part of the decision making process. She often was also part of the selection process for wife number two. The wedding for wife number two could only be done traditionally and legally, because this practice was banned by the Church. She was usually much younger than the first wife, yet the relationship between the wives was apparently cordial. The husband's nights were allocated to each wife in such a way as not to disrupt family equilibrium.

Whenever anything contrary to this pattern happened, there would be no peace in the home.

The church was always full to capacity on Sundays, and beyond capacity on holidays such as Christmas, Easter (Paska), Ascension Day, Pentecost Day, among other major Church holidays. Today, these things seem like fantasy, yet these were the realities of my early childhood environment. They shaped my thinking and my personality.

Also accounting for my extreme naiveté was the fact that my mother and grandmothers had been very protective of my siblings and me. I remember my paternal grandmother explaining to me why she—as well as my mother—had to shave my hair rather than braid it. I wanted to wear braids like many other girls in my age group. She said she was trying to protect me from being molested. Although I was not the only girl being shaved, other kids, especially boys, made fun of my shaven head and they teased me by slapping my head from behind in the classroom. Whenever I turned to see who had slapped me, everybody was pretending to be busy reading. This was done most of my childhood until I went to live with Uncle Nakunu.

My family's mistake was to try to protect me without teaching me how to protect myself. When my age of puberty struck, I was totally unprepared for the dangers ahead of me. For example, I was totally unaware of my good looks, simply because my constantly shaven head, my legs (slightly bowed), and my complexion had been made fun of so much and so often that I became convinced of my utter ugliness. Uncle Nakunu and his wife had let my hair grow freely. A few months later, when people began to talk about my hair and good looks, I could not relate to it. It was as if they were talking about someone I did not know.

On the physical side, I understood that part of my physical weakness was due to the fact that I did not eat the richer foods I needed to eat, such as various types of greens, all types of mushrooms, certain types of meats (the skin, feet and head), and a variety of abundantly available vegetables, but I preferred junk foods, chocolate, candy, and the crust of staple foods, among other non-nutritious food stuff. The adults in my childhood, especially my mother and grandmothers, tried everything to make me eat well, but it did not work, so they left me alone. Thank God my father gave me food supplements, but when I was in the village with my paternal grandmother, I did not take them. Consequently, I was frequently anemic. Also, I did not take enough fluids; namely, I was unable to finish a whole glass of water in one go. As a result, I was frequently dehydrated.

On the stoic side, two major events shaped my mind in a drastic way. I had tended to be a crybaby in my early childhood. I cried for the slightest frustration or discomfort. My parents and grandparents had too many of us to always attend to my bouts of crying, so my siblings and cousins decided to help me cry. They then took the habit of responding to my crying in unison. This made it sound like I was the lead singer, and they were the chorus. This made me upset and I'd cry more furiously. They, too, would pretend to cry just as furiously. Then they would burst out in laughter. The adults let them do this to me because they too were tired of my crying. One day, I decided that they had had enough fun at my expense. I decided that I would not let anybody hear me cry again, ever. I simply stopped crying. No matter how badly I felt like crying, I refused to cry anymore.

The second event was a one-time occurrence in the village. I must have been ten or eleven years old. One hot and sunny afternoon, I was standing at the southern end of my paternal aunt's front yard. There was a bush separating her husband's big house from their neighbors' kitchen house. All of a sudden, I saw the biggest and longest black snake (okóm) I had ever seen. It was crossing the small dirt road, from the west side to the east side. I instantly began to scream in fear. My aunt's husband and other adults came running and asking what was the matter. I answered, pointing my finger toward the reptile "a big snake!"

To my dismay, my aunt's husband began to rebuke me, saying: "You this child, you are strange! How did you manage to see it?!" No one ever mentioned this incident again. It was as if it had never happened! I gathered that it was not a regular snake; namely, it was a totem and I, as an uninitiated, was not supposed to have seen it. Since that day, I never screamed again when facing danger. Could it be that I had become unconsciously afraid to be yelled at for bringing danger on myself?

Whatever the case, I decided that this victimization syndrome was a consequence of the self-sustaining malicious system in which I was born, and I did not have to keep enduring it. Could things change? Yes, things could change for me, but how? I was a young lone woman; it was not such a realistic idea to try to change the system. My thinking was that, although I may not be able to change the system, something had to change. "I'll start with myself," I said. "This endless victimization has got to stop!" My mind was made up.

FORMATION OF A PERSONALITY

Answers to the questions I had asked myself previously about how I had become easy prey to unscrupulous men made me feel empowered. These were mainly gathered from precious childhood memories, current good realities such as my spiritual birth experience, my personal relationship with the Lord, and sad socio-political realities that I felt I could not change, and my dreams for the future. I decided to make some vital adjustments in my inner world. As I made these adjustments, it felt as if I was swimming against a strong current. I knew the Lord would help me, and I prayed a lot. I had to change me.

First, naiveté had to go! I began to pray intensely for the Lord to deliver me from naiveté by granting me one of the gifts of the Holy Spirit, the gift of discernment. Slowly, I began to understand that people do not always mean what they say, and that they sometimes do things without much prior thinking. This made me establish that my trust was to be earned, and not granted instantly as I had tended to do. I also prayed that the Lord would keep me from paranoia, and show me ways to remain loving and caring without being taken advantage of.

The Lord then asked me to forgive everyone who had hurt me, and to surrender my every hurt and fear, my every feeling and desire, along with my mind and my very life, to Him, trusting that He would not fail me. It was a learning process. He taught me how to relate to people, not directly, but through Him and for His sake. I found myself taking ownership of His Word as I increasingly read, memorized, and professed it daily.

I became an avid reader of dietary information. This helped me understand that the best foods are not necessarily my favorites, but the ones that would enhance my body strength. I started eating a wider variety of vegetables and fruits, whether I felt hungry or not. I also drank more liquids, especially water, whether I felt thirsty or not.

Also, one day in March 1987, the Lord healed me miraculously of the dangerously low blood pressure that I had suffered from for eight years. This problem appeared at the time following my father's untimely death when he was just 47 years old. The healing occurred during an evangelistic crusade in Yaounde conducted by an evangelist by the name of J.L. Jayet. All of a sudden, my blood circulation was boosted so much that I got caught up in a laughing bout that lasted more than thirty minutes. All symptoms were gone! I felt very energetic and very happy. I then knew that my future would be bright, and better things were ahead of me. I felt the strongest and happiest that I had felt in my entire life.

I decided to enhance my newly found physical energy with physical exercise, but I was so unaccustomed to exercise that I was unable to do more than two push-ups in a row. Sit-ups were very difficult and painful too. I started with jogging on a flat ground for two kilometers. I then moved on to take the bigger challenge of jogging up and down some of Yaounde's steep hills. After a few successful trials, I went to the Parcours Vita in Mount Febe, a running track in the mountain with stations for all sorts of other physical exercises. The experience was so challenging that I almost passed out the first day. God sent a man along to show me some tricks. For example, he showed me how to breathe rhythmically while jogging or doing push-ups or sit-ups; how to use various parts of leg muscles by running backward when the slope was too challenging; what to do when feeling faint during exercise; and the importance of drinking water. I never saw that man again, but I religiously applied his instructions. After a while, some men began to complain about me being too strong, especially when I shook hands with them. I said, "Me, too strong?!" From then on, anybody who tried to mess with me always had something to say about my physical strength.

For example, when one male acquaintance of mine tried to kiss me by force a few years ago, I twisted his arm and held it firmly behind his back. His attempts to pull out his arm failed. I held it long enough for him to understand that I would do worse if he tried forcing me again. All of sudden, he began to complain about being a weak man. I said, "Uh huh!"

God's power in me has not been limited to my physical empowerment. It is deeper than that. One cold night in early March 1998, I found myself on the Number 7 subway line in Queens, New York, on my way back to Manhattan. I was sitting on the rear car of the train, just so I could conveniently take the exit closest to my home. At one point, a young man, apparently in his mid-to-late twenties, stepped into the car. Automatically, the Spirit of the Lord warned me to be on my guard. He walked past me, to the very end of the car. I noticed from the corner of my eye that he was dropping his trousers. The first thought that came to my mind was, "Is this animal going to pee in here?!" He probably thought I did not see what he had just done. So, he turned to me, his loosed trousers camouflaged by his long winter jacket. He pretended he wanted to know what time it was, and asked me, "Miss, do you have the time?" I did not hesitate one moment, knowing what he was up to. I yelled and jumped at him simultaneously, saying, "How dare you!" Within forty-five seconds or so, he was saying, "I'm sorry, Ma'am! I'm sorry!" and begging me not to pull the emergency brake of the train, which I had threatened to pull. He ran away just as soon as he was able to. Although I was royally disgusted by his attempt, I was happy to see the Lord give me a chance to exercise my spiritual authority over the demons of rape. I was definitely getting my revenge. It felt good to see them tremble! Praise Jesus!

VERTICAL
MOVE

A different type of demon attacked me just three months after my arrival in New York: the demons of mugging. One evening at my office, I got carried away with work, not keeping track of time. By the time I looked at the clock, it was after 9 p.m. I took the Number 3 subway line to Saratoga Avenue in Brownsville, Brooklyn, New York, where I lived at the time. By the time I got off the train, it was after 10. Not too many people in that area were hanging out at this time, except a group of four or six adolescents in front of a public school. I went past them without paying much attention to them. All of a sudden, it occurred to me that I was under assault. Something that had hit me in the back had just dropped on the floor behind me. I turned around to see what it was that had hit me. Instead, I saw these youngsters looking at me, ready to do their evil work.

When I understood what was happening, my spirit just opened up like a parachute. The scriptures, "For we wrestle not against flesh and blood, but against principalities, against powers, against the rulers of darkness of this world, against spiritual wickedness in high places..." (Ephesians 6:12), and "Ye are of God, little children, and have overcome them: because greater is he that is in you, than he that is in the world..." (1 John 4:4), popped in my mind immediately. I wanted to laugh, but the Spirit let me just stare at them, with a big smile on my face, which was a message to the devil. I was telling him, spiritually, that he had failed his coup, because the Lord Jesus in me is greater than all the demons in hell or anywhere else.

The youngsters looked at each other, obviously perplexed, and took off. And I walked to my temporary home in peace. God did not bring me to America to become a murder statistic. That is not going to happen! Anybody with such plans is a failure! I was thrilled to see my attackers take off. The Word of God is really powerful!

Another incident occurred one cold Saturday evening, early January 1997. I was invited to preach at a platform service in a small church in the Bedford-Stuyvesant area of Brooklyn, on Fulton Street. The church doors had not yet been opened, and it was too cold for me to stand wait outside. So, I found refuge in a take out fish fry restaurant. A man, apparently homeless, walked up to me and asked for money for food. I asked him if food was what he really wanted. When he insisted that it was, I told him to choose his meal from the menu, and I would pay. He chose a fish sandwich, and I paid for it. A few minutes later, this man came back to return the sandwich, and get the cash instead. He apparently thought I would have left. From the corner, I watched in silence, hoping that his request would be denied, but it was not. They gave him the money. I stopped the man and demanded that he give me my money back, knowing that he was not going to use my hard earned money for anything good. When he understood that his attempt had failed, he returned the money to me.

Meanwhile, the church had opened its doors, and the service went on well. On my way back to Manhattan by subway, I bumped into this panhandler who was now very angry. He stopped me and said, "Why did you embarrass me before people?" The only answer I was able to offer him was a smile. He kept harassing me until I got off to transfer to an uptown train.

Unfortunately, subway traffic late at night can be difficult. Uptown trains were not stopping at this station. We were asked to take the downtown train to the next station, where we would then be able to take the uptown train. This man kept following me around. By the time I got to the desired station, there was just the two of us there, and it was very late. He stood in front of me, nose to nose, eyeball to eyeball, apparently determined to do me harm.

At this point I got tired of him, and said to him, "Sir, I do not owe you anything! I simply took my money back from you because you lied to me. And for your information, you do not scare me! Second, I do not want to hurt you. So, do not force me to hurt you!" He kept standing there, staring at me. After about two or so minutes, he finally left.

Some may think I was bluffing, but those who know the God of Elijah and Elisha will perfectly understand that I was far from bluffing.

The Word of God is true, and I believe in, and use the authority of the mighty name of Jesus Christ wherever I find myself, at anytime of the day or the night. I shall not be intimidated by demons or people or animals or things!
Luke 10:19–20

The more I read, memorized, and meditated on the Word, the more I understood its implications for my daily life. As my understanding of my spiritual nature increased, it occurred to me that, although I grew up a religious child, I had been spiritually dead, and that most of the things that had happened to me were a result of my spiritual death. *Having now surrendered my all to the Lord, and dwelling in His Word, and depending on it, I was full of life, peace, joy, and strength and authority, inside out. No more fear! No more naiveté! No more victimization!*

I now know that my natural person cannot help but practice sin, no matter how good the intensions. When I neglected to gain nourishment from the Word of God in my earlier youth, my spiritual malnourishment and subsequent weakness rivaled my physical malnourishment and weakness. This explains why I was easily victimized by circumstances *and people. I can understand the things of God's Kingdom only through my spirit. The intellect is just like a computer screen on which the interpretation of the messages that God deposits in our spirit are received.*

As my spirit was dead, all I had at the time was the intellect, which is too weak to understand the things of the Living God. This knowledge has set me free, just as the Lord Jesus promised it would: "Then said Jesus to those Jews which believed on him, if ye continue in my word, then are ye my disciples indeed: And ye shall know the truth, and the truth shall make you free." John 8:31–32. *My spiritual freedom came only when I embraced the Word of God and obeyed it wholeheartedly.*

Although it was hard at times, I obeyed the Word when it commanded me to forgive what I considered unforgivable. In such instances, I prayed, asking the Lord for the strength to forgive. And He helped me to do so through the power of His Holy Spirit. *By forgiving the wicked, I am now free from bitterness and hate. In fact, praying for the salvation of all my human oppressors has become a daily reality in my life.* It was one of the most exciting things to see one of my former oppressors turn to Christ. Indescribable peace and joy has now replaced my former bitterness.

I now possess an unshakable assurance of salvation. There is not one shadow of a doubt in my mind that God loves me, and I love Him back with every fiber of my being. *Jesus set me free from bitterness and depression. Glory to His holy and mighty name!*

I have been delivered from a victim's frame of mind to one of a victorious soldier in the earthly Army of the Lord. I do not hate my body anymore. I now appreciate and take good care of every physical attribute the Lord gave me. Yes, I hated my body as well as my being a female, because many of my assailants gave my physical attributes as their excuse for sexually assaulting me. For a long time, I would freak out if a man told me I was sexy. The phrase "You are sexy" was absolutely scary to me. Back then, people talked excitedly about my hair, but I did not mind cutting it. Women said I was wasting such beautiful hair. Of course they did not know what I had endured because of it.

Elsewhere, I may have appeared as brown skin, but to my people I was light. According to their preferences, such attributes made a woman attractive. It was to the point where many females bleached their skin in order to appear light. However, being physically attractive was a torture to me. I tried physical neglect, but that did not help. As the Lord led me through the inner healing process, it became increasingly clear that God made me exactly the way I look, and all that God made is good. He did it for His glory, not for what unscrupulous and undisciplined men had turned it into. I finally accepted my physical attributes as being good, and took ownership of them.

One of the toughest things was to accept my being a woman as a good thing. I had been held down by society—not my parents—because I was a woman. I hated the lies that were sold to women in the name of femininity. My thinking was that, while young girls were barred from acquiring certain skills necessary for their survival, they were released into society, totally unprepared for the rough road ahead of them. I then took to envying men because, at the time, I thought they were rape free. Society seemed to belong all to them. They were entitled to so much: self defense, freedom of movement (no man seemed to need his wife's permission to travel while the opposite was not true, at the time) and freedom of expression, among other privileges.

However, the Lord, through His Word, and also through my professional training, helped me to see a different picture of women and men.

The first time I found that little boys, and grown men, also get raped or sexually assaulted, but they are too proud to tell, I was absolutely astounded. Through His Word, the Lord taught me that He made man first and woman next. And this too was good, and for His glory. I then decided that the gender situation, as I had experienced it, was a distortion of God's Plan. God destined us all for greatness, but our spiritual deadness has kept us bound in the tyranny of self-centeredness, self and mutual destruction.

I praise the Lord that I have now taken ownership of my femininity. I thank God for making me a woman.

And I happily celebrate Women's Day at my church and anywhere else. Only Jesus could have done this in me. Glory to His holy name!

THE
TURNING
POINT

Early in the year 2003, I received an invitation to go
and minister in Yaounde, Cameroon as one of the
guest speakers at the Christ's Reformed Assembly's
annual convention. It was a bit difficult. I had been
living far from my country for more than 13 years
and now an invitation asked me to go back where I
had started in the ministry and subsequently been
rejected. I prayed and fasted, and God confirmed
that it was His will. I began to prepare myself for my
first official invitation to my homeland as a minister
of God.

On the evening of the first day of March, my
plane landed at the Yaounde, Nsimalen International Airport. When I arrived, I felt great joy, mixed
with some apprehension. I saw the many people
who had come with a fleet of cars to welcome me at
the Airport. Bishop Honoré Mbiakang, the leader
of the convention, and Apostle Abraham Achilles
Mendogo, a son of mine in the Lord (who had in-

troduced me to Bishop Mbiakang), along with many other clergy and church leaders, had come. My elder sister Marie-Louise Abila, my junior brothers Paul M.D. Abila Assomo and Pastor Guy Eyebe with their wives, along with a host of friends such as Emilienne Ononino-Ze among others, and family members, had also come. This was the first time I had experienced such a situation. I was feeling a strong sense of destiny inside of me. This, and the events that followed during my trip, confirmed my feeling that this was happening by divine appointment.

Although I was unable to accept all the invitations to preach, I did minister in different churches. I gave my testimony and lifted up the name of Jesus Christ. God broke through and many lives were transformed by the power of the Holy Spirit. As I prayed in my hotel room, God kept confirming the fact that a new door of ministry was opened to me.

God has given me compassion for the suffering. Wherever (and whenever) I get a chance, I tell people what God has done for me. It doesn't matter how deep our troubles are, or how low we fall, God loves us. And if we give Him a chance, He will reveal Himself to us. He will bless us, and transform our lives in unimaginable ways. What He did for me, He is able and willing to do for anybody who dares to believe in His Word.

The question is: How badly do you want to come out of your hole? You see, some people give up on themselves. Others may give up on you, but you do not have to give up on yourself! Have you given up on yourself? I hope not. If you have, then I encourage you to give God a chance. He is real! There is a great destiny waiting for you out there. Just make Jesus your personal Lord and Savior, and He will guide and lead you into your great destiny. You are destined for greatness!

God is love, and love is powerful. It does not matter who abused you, or how many times. It does not matter how big the problem is. God is willing and able to fix it for you, if you give Him a chance. God loves you!

The Lord has put it in my heart to share what He has done for me with the whole world. He has broken my chains and bestowed many blessings upon me, not to keep it to myself, but to open myself up to those who have lost all hope. To them I would like to reach out and say, there is hope in Jesus Christ. He did it for me. He will do the same for anybody who believes in Him, and will offer Him the throne of their heart. I am no longer the same. All who knew me back then can attest to this. Glory to the name of the Lord for ever!

I now understand the Scriptures of the Apostle Paul, who declares: "Here is a trustworthy saying that deserves full acceptance: Christ Jesus came into the world to save sinners—of whom I am the worst. But for that very reason I was shown mercy so that in me, the worst of sinners, Christ Jesus might display his unlimited patience as an example for those

who would believe on him and receive eternal life."
(1Timothy 1:15–16)

I pray that my testimony would serve everywhere
to inspire and guide bruised souls and broken hearts
toward the Lord Jesus Christ, who gave His very life
as a sacrifice to give another chance to sinners. Because of His ultimate sacrifice for us, He is the only
one who can truly heal a broken heart. My burning
desire is to see millions of people see in me an example of divine grace and mercy, for their own inspi-
ration and salvation. "... He is patient with you, not
wanting anyone to perish, but everyone to come to
repentance." (2 Peter 3: 9b)

I SHALL NOT SCREAM!

LOOKING BACK ON MY JOURNEY FROM DEATH TO LIFE

When I became pregnant the first time, I started with selling roasted peanuts in the street, at Avenue Germaine, a popular junction in the north-east side of Yaounde. Then I graduated to selling fruits and doughnuts, until I passed my secondary school certificate through evening classes at Institut Samba. This certificate qualified me for a government job that earned less than $50 per month. In my attempts to climb out of severe poverty, and as the demons of poverty kept creating havoc in my life, I became more and more depressed and collapsed inside. I could not sleep no matter how tired I felt. I began to feel a strong impulse to scream. Then a voice kept telling me to scream. I knew if I gave in, I would become completely psychotic, and it would be difficult for me to find my way back to my right mind. So, I decided to confront this voice. I asked the voice, "You keep telling me to scream, but who are you, and what is your name?" No answer came. Then I said, "I'm not going to scream either." That was the last time I heard this voice. Today, I realize that it was God's grace at work in me, giving me the strength to resist the devil. To Him be glory and honor and praise, for ever!

And yet, as I continued to feel drained, I dropped out of my evening classes in the very year I was supposed to graduate. Someone mentioned the term brain fatigue. Then another mentioned an emotional weakness.

Upon following the advice of well meaning acquaintances who thought I needed companionship, I started looking for friends and began to go out after work and on Saturday nights. Then I became horrified by the excessive drinking of my new found friends. The next thing I knew, I was telling them I hated their smoking and drinking and dirty talk. They could tell I was a naïve girl with a strong religious background. They smooth talked me into hanging out with them again. In a short time, I had become so corrupt that I became addicted to smoking cigarettes and began to drift into pornography. At this time I was a little better off financially; my salary had doubled after my advanced certificate. But I was still relatively poor.

Now my struggle was no longer just against poverty and depression, but also against sexual perversion. Sexual demons are tenacious. I had to quickly cry out to Jesus as I felt like I was being swallowed up into something that I did not want to be. I learned to depend on Jesus Christ for strength to come, and stay, out of cigarettes and pornography. With His help, I cut my relationships with the company that pushed me into these vices, and enabled them. It was a long and torturous process.

But through it all, I learned not to trust myself, and to depend on the power of the Word of God to live right. After a few years, I was totally delivered from both vices. I have grown increasingly stronger with time. God is faithful enough to lead us to our final destination. God alone, through His Son Jesus Christ alone, is worthy of my trust, not people!

Now that I was free from these chains, I was able to return to school, just as soon as the Lord made a way for it. Of course it was a struggle to re-acquaint my brain with mathematics and other challenging subjects. I then learned to make wiser use of the twenty-four hours God gives each one of us daily. By then I was really blessed spiritually and financially. I was advancing in ministry, and could afford a nice car, a nice vacation, nice clothes and other niceties of life. However, I decided to pursue higher learning through the theological seminary and the university. All my studies were paid out of my pocket, with the exception of a little help I received from my employer in my university studies (50 percent of tuition and books for courses deemed relevant to my job were reimbursed to me at the end of every semester, when applicable). My efforts were rewarded with the knowledge I acquired and the degrees I earned.

When I became born again, I was still making approximately $50 per month, that is almost $600 per year. I was told that God expected me to support His work financially through tithing and sacrificial giving. I was shocked initially, because I was making so little. How could I then even consider tithing! However, I accepted the challenge, and obeyed God's Word anyway.

This year (1981) turned out to be a year of financial breakthrough. I passed my advanced certificate, and my salary doubled as a result. That motivated me to keep on tithing and give even more. Today, I am blessed. I believe my tithing and sacrificial giving to God's work, both in my church and other ministries as well as to support the poor and needy, has something to do with my being blessed today. That is why I encourage believers to tithe and give generously and sacrificially to God. As I gained more understanding of the principle of stewardship, namely that I and everything I have belong to God, I gave my all to Him, including my talents, skills, and other abilities. This has contributed in the improvement of all aspects of my life.

I could have settled for less, as many people in my condition did. There were very dark moments. Many times I was tempted to give up and kill myself. Yet God, who knew me even when I was not yet saved, kept putting in me the desire for greatness and excellence.

Now the former street vendor of roasted peanuts has been blessed with homeownership (though modest) in my country of nationality and in my country of residence, among other blessings.

One of my biggest blessings came about when the Word of God invaded my spirit, mind, and soul, and delivered me from the ugliest demon in my life, that is, depression. I know for myself that *depression is an ugly and stubbornly persistent demon.* This one took so long to get rid of. But with Jesus and His Word in me, I swallowed up depression and it did not swallow me up! ALLELUIA!

I now take pleasure in helping other people suffering from depression, especially the suffering, to overcome their demons in Jesus' name and with His Word. GLORY BE TO JEHOVAH NISSI!

Although I have been consistently blessed by my God, I do not consider myself arrived. There are still many barriers in my life to break, many mountains to move, and more blessings are coming my way. *I am not in the Promised Land yet. The Promised Land is The Heavenly Jerusalem. Nothing I have here on earth could compare to my heavenly destiny.* I look at my life as a constant warfare with specific battles. As I look back over my life, I just see the mighty hand of God keeping me and blessing me. And I know for myself day and night, rain, snow, and sunshine, that He did not bring me this far to leave me. He did not keep me alive just so I could be destroyed by some demonic force. No, I don't think so! I now face my battles with more confidence than ever before.

My friend, God knows you so well! He has prepared something special for you. Only you can fulfill it. You are destined for greatness! God has prepared a great destiny for you. *Although God has this great destiny for you, He will not force you to reach it.* You need to believe this! With the Lord Jesus Christ on your side, the devil and all of the world systems are not powerful enough to keep you from reaching your glorious destiny. Only you can decide not to be great. I hope you will decide to choose Jesus Christ over yourself!

When circumstances firmly stood against me, I became suicidal at times. And when temptations came to just end it all, I wanted to throw in the towel, but I would think about my sons. I was the only parent they had. They needed me so much.

Selfishness is a terrible thing. Had I lived for myself, I would have killed myself. But because I lived for others (initially for my children and my family, and later on for God), I had to go on living, believing God, and trusting that He will make a way, somehow. He sure enough did.

The possibilities are in you. You see, if God has allowed you to live, it is because He has a lot for you. He has a lot of love and power for you to enjoy! You must give him a chance. He will show you the possibilities in you that you have not been able to see so far, probably because of adverse circumstances in your life.

Today I sing and play music for the Lord. Who could have told me in those days that I would be a singer for Jesus? Only He could bring out the singer in me!

JESUS, THE ONLY WAY OUT!

Many are unemployed. To them I say, learn to seize all the opportunities God is bringing your way. If you do not have a job, find something to do, and trust God for an increase.

I started out as a street vendor selling roasted peanuts to prepare for the birth of my first son. Later on I graduated to selling fruits and dumplings or donuts. With this, I was able to keep my dignity and take care of my babies. You can do the same, and God will prosper you.

I know many people are traumatized and are desperate for help. Some are affected by horrible memories of war whereby they witnessed their loved ones being killed. Some have lost their minds or fallen into all sorts of addictions. Others suffered physical traumas that affect their emotions and personality in a profound way. I think of the direct victims of September 11, who must now deal with the horrible memories. I know, for a fact, that there is hope for inner healing and peace in Jesus. Just give God a chance to prove this to you!

Victims of physical and emotional torture abound throughout the world. Others are repeatedly raped in their prison cells, common bathrooms, and other settings. Many homosexuals live under the burdens of shame and fear. Many have been pushed into prostitution and other dangerous lifestyles, and they cannot find their way out. They are prisoners of the mountains that stand firmly against them. *Despair and unbelief have made them blind to the fact that God is bigger than their difficulties.* He is able to make a way for you even when there seems to be no way. Jesus is the way out of any hole or any nightmarish situation. Just give God a chance to prove this to you! "The true light that gives light to every man was coming into the world." (John 1:9)

People need peace and enlightenment. Many are thirsty for love. The thirst for love and acceptance has led many youths and adults into gangs, occultism, pornography, and drug addiction. But none of these precious things can really be found where we usually look for them. Jesus is the true Love and Light. I know this for myself.

Jesus is the Light that will enlighten your existence and remove the darkness that came into it as the result of self-centeredness and selfishness, which I consider to be the root of sin and its consequences.

GOD MEANS BUSINESS. He is reaching out to you today. If you accept Him, He will heal your bruised soul, and satisfy your longing for love and peace. He will change your circumstances, and totally transform your inner being. I know because He did it for me. I am very satisfied in Him! No more depression! No more suicidal tendencies! No more sleepless nights! No more fear! I now know Jesus for myself. He has delivered me from the overwhelming feelings of helplessness and despair that used to push me into self-pity and depression. The Spirit of the Lord is now a joyful, peaceful, and powerful reality in my life. Alleluia!

In those very poor days, often times I could not afford to buy a can of sardines and bread. To avoid falling into the trap of frustration and compromise, I would think of my future, how it would be so great, and I will be able to buy many cans of sardines and loaves of bread. Now by God's grace I can buy many boxes of sardines and loaves of bread, if I wanted to.

You can choose to reorganize your life and, as you incorporate new Christ-centered habits into it, God will promote you. It was not easy for the Lord Jesus to go to the cross and be crucified to save us from our sins and their consequences. He had to suffer indescribable pain and humiliations, as well as immeasurable agony, to give us access to Eternal Life and set us free from all the powers of darkness. Because of what the Lord Jesus suffered on our behalf, we have become men and women of great destiny. It does not matter where in the social landscape you find yourself at this moment; I want you to know that you are destined for greatness!

Unfortunately, we have a determined enemy, Satan, who is working very hard at turning our great destiny into horror, poverty, and damnation. The good news is, Satan can only succeed in his work of destruction in your life if you let him. Do not let your circumstances intimidate you! With the Lord Jesus on your side, you can, and you will, overcome each and every one of your adverse circumstances, if you trust Him. You will then be able to reach and enjoy your great destiny. *With persistent faith in the Word of God, we can move the mountains of adverse circumstances out of our way.*

FIRST BAPTIST CHURCH OF BROWNSVILLE, INC.

357 CHESTER STREET • P.O. BOX 146 • BROOKLYN, N.Y. 11212

CHAIRMAN OF DEACON BOARD
DEACON CLARENCE WHITAKER
(718) 531-6312
OFFICE (718) 498-1074 /1337
FAX (718) 345-2822

CHAIRMAN OF TRUSTEE BOARD
SISTER YVONNE MARKS
(516) 868-2808
KITCHEN (718) 498-1097

OVERSEER A.D. LYON, PASTOR
CHURCH CLERK: SISTER LYDIA LINDSAY
E-MAIL: Lyonfbcb@worldnet.att.net

May 27, 2003

Minister Mengue Eka-Abila, joined in fellowship with First Baptist Church in May of 1990. She then later united with the church in September of that same year.

Min. Mengue as we call her, has continuously showed dedicated service in all that she does. In 1992 she served as Youth director until 1996 when her title was changed to youth minister were she served until 1999.

Min. Mengue now heads our Street Evangelism Ministry and is part of our Associate Ministers staff. She serves as an Altar Worker and is a Teacher in our Sunday school and is on the Praise team.

Min. Mengue is one who loves to Praise and Worship the Lord. She brings joy to all who watch, as she demonstrates Praise in dance, just as David did when the Ark of the Lord was returned to Jerusalem. There is only one like her.

Because of Calvary,

Bishop-Designate A.D. Lyon
Bishop - Designate A.D. Lyon, Pastor

ADL:dw

FORGET THE WORD EASY